# BEAUTY AND THE BEAST

CHARLES PERRAULT

Once upon a time, there lived a very wealthy merchant. He owned many ships which sailed to all of the exciting lands of the world. These ships went to India for fine silks, to South America for gold and to England for iron and tin.

This merchant had three daughters and they all lived in a rich, huge castle.

The merchant loved all three of his daughters. But the youngest, called Beauty, was his favorite. She was beautiful, not only because she had a lovely face, but because she was also kind and good.

One night, the merchant and his daughters were having their dinner, when a messenger suddenly burst into the room.

Please pardon me, sir. I have sad news for you.

What is it?

"A frightful storm at sea has caused your ships to sink. All of your riches are lost. You are a poor man."

In a single night, the merchant was reduced from riches to poverty. No longer could he live in the huge castle with many servants. He and his daughters moved to a small, poor cottage.

Beauty did not weep at her change of fortune. The loss of jewels and fine clothing did not cause her any pain. She was as sweet and as kind as ever.

She had always loved flowers, so she planted her own garden. All kinds of flowers bloomed there . . . except roses.

I have tried to grow roses so often, but they always vanish so strangely. I hope that someday I shall have a beautiful garden of roses.

**B**ut Beauty's pleasure in her new life was not shared by her sisters.

**T**hey refused to help her with housework.

**A**nd they blamed their father for their poor clothing and loss of fine jewelry.

**T**hey were miserable. And because they were miserable, they grew ugly. Their faces became wrinkled with frowns and the corners of their mouths turned down. But Beauty, because she was happy, became more beautiful than ever.

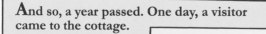

And so, a year passed. One day, a visitor came to the cottage.

Sir, I bring you good news. One of the ships that we thought was lost in the great storm last year has arrived in port. You are once again a wealthy man.

Daughters - - do you hear that? We are rich again! I will go to the port tomorrow to claim one of my ships which did not sink last year.

Now we can have pretty jewels!

And fine clothing and a great house!

What is wrong, Beauty? You don't seem to be happy with my good fortune.

I like it so well here. I am sad that we will soon be leaving.

Ah, Beauty, you will be happier in a fine house with servants and beautiful things. Now, tell me, daughters, what presents shall I bring you when I return from my journey?

Bring me a watch made with diamonds, bracelets of the most precious gems and a crown of rubies. You may also bring me . . .

Wait, sister. You will ruin our father before it comes to my turn. I only ask for a few of the most splendid Persian turbans, some dresses of the richest lace and two or three shawls of the finest wool.

Well, Beauty, and what do you wish?

I wish for nothing but your safe return, Father.

No, child, you must make a request.

Then, since they won't grow in my garden; bring me a rose.

The following morning, the merchant left on his journey.

After the merchant took care of his business, he bought the presents for his two older daughters and started for home.

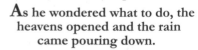

Toward evening, he reached a forest.

The forest was dark and stormy. Soon . . .

I am lost. I don't know which way to go.

As he wondered what to do, the heavens opened and the rain came pouring down.

After a few moments, a sweet sound was heard.

On, merchant, on! Your journey's nearly done.

At that instant, a small blue light appeared through the trees. The merchant rode toward the light.

The light became a large flame, and then disappeared. In its place stood the gates of a magnificent palace.

ENTER WITHOUT FEAR FOR ALL ARE WELCOME HERE

The gates suddenly opened without a sound. Although no one was to be seen, the merchant entered the courtyard and dismounted. His horse at once trotted off toward the stable, as though it knew the way.

When the merchant followed the horse to the stable, he found it all groomed and cleaned, feeding on oats and hay. But still, no one was to be seen.

The merchant left the stable and went across the courtyard into a brightly lit hallway. As he passed a door, it swung open.

He entered and saw fine clothing spread before a blazing fire. But wet and weary as he was, he was afraid to touch anything. Then he heard another sweet voice.

You are a guest for tonight and all that is right, will appear to your sight, to be used without fright.

After bathing, the merchant dressed in the dry clothing he found. Then he walked down the hall until another door swung open into a huge dining room.

As he finished each course, the empty plates were removed by unseen hands.

When he was finished, another door opened into a bedroom. Before going to sleep, the merchant offered grateful thanks for his shelter.

The next morning, after breakfast, the merchant strolled through the gardens searching for a rose to bring Beauty. But just as he plucked one of the lovely flowers . . .

That evening, the merchant reached his cottage. Beauty ran to meet him.

Father, why do you look so sad?

Here, my child, take the rose you asked for.

As the merchant gave Beauty the rose, a strange thing happened.

Why, Father, the rose is blooming in my hand. What magic is this?

Come into the cottage, child. I shall tell you all that has happened.

A few minutes later, Beauty had heard the strange story.

Father, you must not return to the castle. You took the rose because of me. Therefore, I shall go in your place.

But you may be in great danger there.

Your life is more important than mine. You must stay here to take care of my sisters.

Just then, the two elder sisters burst into the room.

Well, Father, where are my bracelets, my watch, my crown of rubies?

Where are my turbans, my dresses, my shawls?

Please, sisters, do not trouble Father now. He is very sad.

Sad? Did he bring our jewelry and clothing?

Yes, sisters, he brought them.

If he brought our presents, how can he be sad?

Beauty then told them about the rose.

You wicked child, asking for a rose! Why, you might have caused us to lose our jewelry and clothing!

What a risk for a simple rose! Let us throw it into the fire!

16

**S**he tried to seize the rose. But as she reached for it, it flew away and . . .

. . . took refuge with Beauty.

**T**he astonished sisters realized that the rose was enchanted and they promised never again to touch it.

**T**he week passed quickly and the morning for the departure came. The merchant insisted on taking his daughter to the Beast's palace.

**A**s they reached the palace, the gates flew open.

The merchant went to his room. further down the hall, there was a place for Beauty.

As she touched the knob, the door swung open. Beauty stood there breathless at the sight which greeted her.

Beauty entered and sank into a chair, afraid to touch anything. Then she heard a sweet voice.

Welcome, Beauty. Have no fear. Live as a queen while you are here.

**B**eauty bathed and dressed. Then she met her father in the dining room. There they ate a fine dinner.

**T**hen a voice was heard . . .

The Beast is near and wishes to appear.

I tremble at his coming.

Appear, Beast!

**A**s the Beast approached, Beauty looked at his face and turned away in horror.

Merchant, you have kept your word. I shall try to make Beauty's time here pass pleasantly. She can have all she desires here.

The Beast's voice surprised Beauty. It was not harsh or unpleasant. It was sweet and musical. Beauty looked up, but the strange face caused her to turn away again.

I am sorry, merchant, but you cannot stay here with Beauty. You must leave in the morning.

The following morning . . .

Goodby, Beauty. Be brave.

Don't worry about me, Father.

At first, Beauty felt terribly unhappy. But soon the wonders of the Beast's palace began to enchant her. There were . . .

gardens filled with beautiful flowers and bushes,

lakes filled with gold and silver fish,

a boat that sailed itself

and much, much more.

Beauty had everything she wanted. But she had no one to talk to. She was very, very lonely.

She was so lonely, in fact, that she was happy when she heard voice say . . .

The Beast is near and wishes to appear.

Appear, Beast!

Though she wanted to see him, Beauty could not help trembling with horror when he approached.

Please do not turn from me, Beauty. I will not harm you.

As the beast spoke, Beauty became less afraid. She was almost sorry when evening came.

Now I must leave. Goodnight.

Each day, Beauty looked forward to seeing the Beast.

The Beast is near and wishes to appear.

Oh, yes. Appear, Beast!

Because he was gentle and wise, Beauty soon forgot that he was so strange in appearance.

And when the Beast said farewell each night, Beauty felt sad and longed for the new day.

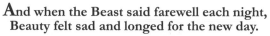

Goodnight, Beauty. Rest well.

Goodnight, gentle Beast. I shall see you tomorrow.

Thus, pleasantly and happily, a half-year passed.

Then one evening, the Beast suddenly took Beauty's hand in his.

Surprised, Beauty pulled her hand away. With a deep, sad sigh, the Beast left.

Goodnight, dear Beauty.

Several days later, the Beast again took Beauty's hand in his.

Beauty, will you marry me?

Oh, no!

The Beast groaned as though his heart was breaking, and he ran from the room.

The next day, the Beast did not come. Nor did he come the following day.

What can this mean? Will I never see him again? Oh, I do hope he comes soon.

As she spoke . . .

Good evening, Beauty.

Oh, Beast, I am so glad you are here.

They spoke of many things that evening. When the Beast rose to leave . . .

I do hope you will come tomorrow.

If you want me, I shall come.

He is so kind and gentle. But I cannot marry him.

All of this time, Beauty did not forget her father and sisters. One day, as she walked through the castle . . .

I wish that I could see what my father is doing now.

As the picture faded from the mirror, the Beast came in.

Beauty, what is the matter?

I have just seen my old home in the mirror. My father seems to be very ill.

You want to visit him, don't you?

Oh, yes, dear Beast.

Take this rose. It is the same one your father plucked when he first came here. As long as you have it, any wish you speak aloud will be granted.

Oh, thank you, Beast! Thank you!

There is only one thing I ask. Do not stay away longer than one week. Please! Even that will seem long without you.

I promise you I shall return within that time. Thank you, dear Beast, and farewell. Now, I wish to be home.

Well, Beauty, It's about time you came home.

How is father? Is he very ill?

Yes, he is. He became sick because he worried about you so much. He has been so sad that he refuses to move out of this horrible cottage into a fine castle where we belong.

I must go to him!

Dear Father!

Beauty! My Beauty! It is good to see you again.

Within two days, the joy of seeing Beauty made the merchant well. But her sisters cared less for Beauty than they cared for the wonders of the Beast's palace which she described to them.

Two nights before the end of the week, the eldest sister decided she would like to go to the palace. She took Beauty's rose and . . .

I wish to be at the Beast's palace.

The rose immediately withered. Instead of taking her to the palace, it threw her into the pigpen.

Help! Help!

Beauty's sister ran from the friendly pigs, back into the cottage. But the rose lay where it had fallen.

The following day, Beauty discovered that her enchanted rose was missing.

Has anyone seen my rose?

No, Beauty, I have not seen it.

Nor I.

Don't ask me. I haven't seen it.

Beauty searched everywhere, but she could not find the rose. Four anxious days passed before she finally saw it on the rubbish heap.

Beauty quickly said farewell to her father and sisters. Then . . .

I wish to be back at the Beast's palace.

At the palace, Beauty waited for the Beast to appear. But he did not come. The day passed, and still Beauty saw no sign of him.

Then, before Beauty's startled eyes, the Beast disappeared. In his place stood one of the handsomest princes in all the wide, wonderful world.

Dear Beauty, your poor Beast was in truth a Prince. I was once bewitched by an evil fairy. She forced me to remain a Beast until I could find someone who would marry me in my horrible form.

A good fairy gave me the magic rose bush. She said it would save me from my frightful curse. And, you see, it has.

The Prince and Beauty were married that very day. And they lived forever after in great happiness.

The End.

**AESOP'S FABLES**
**THE DOG AND THE SHADOW**

There once was a greedy dog who stole a piece of meat from a butcher shop.

I'll take it down to the stream where no one will catch me with it.

Why, that dog in the water has a bigger piece of meat than I have. I want that piece, too.

But as soon as he opened his mouth to snatch at the other piece . . .

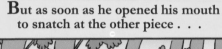

And so the greedy dog was left with nothing.

# RIDE A COCK-HORSE

Ride a cock-horse to Banbury Cross,
To see an old lady upon a white horse;
Rings on her fingers and bells on her toes,
She shall have music wherever she goes.

Ride a cock-horse to Banbury Cross,
To see what Tommy can buy.
A penny white loaf, a penny white cake,
And a two-penny apple pie!

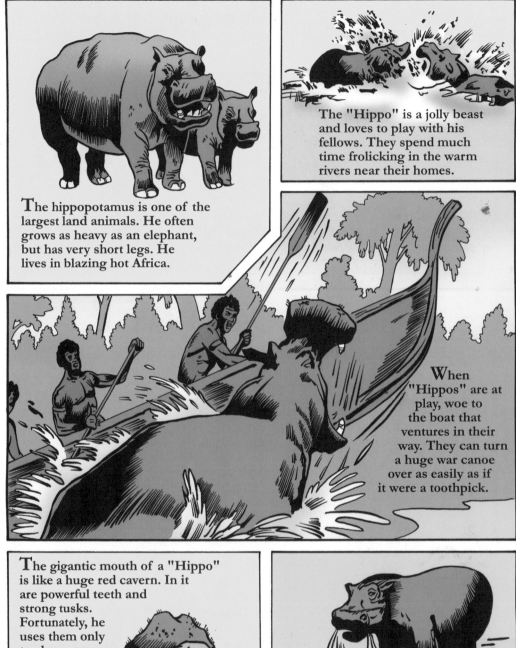

The hippopotamus is one of the largest land animals. He often grows as heavy as an elephant, but has very short legs. He lives in blazing hot Africa.

The "Hippo" is a jolly beast and loves to play with his fellows. They spend much time frolicking in the warm rivers near their homes.

When "Hippos" are at play, woe to the boat that ventures in their way. They can turn a huge war canoe over as easily as if it were a toothpick.

The gigantic mouth of a "Hippo" is like a huge red cavern. In it are powerful teeth and strong tusks. Fortunately, he uses them only to chew grass and hay.

Our friend the "Hippo" has a tiny cousin, the pygmy hippopotamus. He weighs only about one fourteenth as much as his fat cousin. He is not often found as he is shy and likes to keep to himself.